Holy Mess of a Girl

Holy Mess of a Girl

Poems by

J.V. Foerster

Author's photo by Robert Carpenter, photographer
Design support by Glenn Harvey, designer, illustrator
Cover image by Unsplash John Tyson

ISBN: 978-1-63980-395-8
Library of Congress Control Number: 2023941806

Kelsay Books
502 South 1040 East, A-119
American Fork, Utah 84003
Kelsaybooks.com

For Barton and Dr. Tom
Thank you for your gift of healing

Acknowledgments

Thank you to the following publications, where versions of these poems previously appeared:

Agnieszka's Dowry: "The First Temptation Denied"
Amethyst Review: "When the Raven Came"
Blue Bird Word: "Black Lines"
Burningwood Literary Journal: "A Thousand Pieces of My Heart"
Cirque: "Lost at Sea"
Eclectica: "White Swans"
Elohi Gaduji: "The House That You Built for Me," "Untangled"
Fiery Scribe: "Connected," "The Humming Light"
Fifty over Fifty Anthology Philadelphia Stories: "Apple Girl"
Fox Chase Review: "Apple Girl," "The Waves of the Bay," "Do You Know How Dangerous It Is"
Green Ink Poetry Deep Earth Collections Furrows: "The Light of Home at the End of the Gravel Road"
Niederngasse: "Daughter of Enigma"
Oak Bend Review and Concelebratory Shoehorn Review: "Moonlight"
Orchard Lea Anthology Up Close: "My Father Is the Moon Tonight"
The Poetry Field Guide: "A Stone," "Of Mercy and Mercilessness," "A Widow Waiting," "Requiem"
Premiere Generation Ink #5: "Death Toll (My Mother's Miscarriage)," "The Understanding"
Quartet Journal: "Requiem"
Red River Review: "When Angels Sing," "Wash Away the Poet in Me"
Southern Ocean Review: "The Harvest"
Woman Writers Online: "Your Steady Partner"

Deep gratitude to everyone who supported me. It all started with my first poetry teacher/writer Dennis DePauw who read my work, challenged me and opened my world to poetry. Special thanks to Kelli Russell Agodon, Alison Stone, and Tricia Snell for reading my manuscript, supporting me and writing the blurbs. Thanks to Tricia Snell and the writer's group for jump starting me again to finish the book. Thanks, Jim Valentino, for always being there for me and for helping with cover design. Thanks to my cousin/sister Deb Lundstrom for support and editing help.

Miss you everyday Jim Moore, you still are my sunshine. Deeply grateful to my forever friend, Glenn Harvey for helping me decide the cover by using his talent to design endless samples for me.

With gratitude to my mother who gave me nursery rhymes and music. My father gave me the ability to laugh often and see the world with wonder.

All my love to my lost sons, I miss you every day, but thanks for setting me free to be me.

Contents

Black Lines

*Her wings are cut and then she is blamed
for not knowing how to fly.*
                        —Simone de Beauvoir

I imagine my body
free from its bones
the wind my invisible sister.

Free from waking up
and weighing myself
each morning to see what place

I have on the ground in
this world of obsession
to form and insolence.

I dreamed last night that birds
were flying at me and behind them
they left lines in the air.

Thin black lines to hang up my
desires or to dry out my regret.
I think they came to show

me that when the eye can no longer
find its place in the ordinary you
just sleep and dream another life.

The First Temptation Denied

I have never had an appetite
for fruit.
I do not have a season that comes
upon me
where I feel like Eve &
must indulge.
Rather I am a rooted girl
give me the dark hard fibrous life
the strange smell of soil &
the black tint of earth
beneath my nails.
Lusty, rich and swollen
is how I have lived
life.
To me the fruit eaters
thin, transparent, pensive,
are on the edge
of a sick sweet precipice
& below
very shallow waters.

Apple Girl

My grandmother's house always smelled
like apples. Apple kuchen, applesauce,
apple peels. Sweet smell of her soft home.

My mother hated the smell of apples.
My grandma confessed it was
because when she was pregnant with my mother
she climbed the apple trees and ate the tiny green
apples before they were ripe,

The village women stirred up a storm about
that young farmer's wife full of her first child
being crazy and barefoot up those trees.

Among the gentle mother apple trees
cool green hands in the summer's heat.
A young girl clutching pearls of green in her apron
sneaking them home to eat them with salt.

I always believed it was the seeds
a tiny seed that planted itself deep in her body.
Warm, snug the fetus grew and grew
drinking for nine months
the nectar of sour green apples.

Tired of the culture of apples my mother
came out 12 pounds with screaming fists
of insanity
holding apple leaves sticky with juice.

Death Toll

(My Mothers Miscarriage)

In the village where I was born
the church bells rang
when someone died
and we counted the tolls
to tell their age.

Grandmother always knew
when someone died.
She heard a knock
on the door
in the middle of the night
and no one was there.
Or later when she had a phone
it would ring one time
that's all.

Working in her garden
lacy dill stalks taller than me.
Zinnias pop pop color
pink, purple, yellow orange.
Picking the cucumbers
she bent down to give birth to the harvest.

Then the bell
One
We stopped
stood motionless
no wind, no birds,
no more rings.

I scanned the trees
holding my breath
ready to count.
Waiting waiting
Silence stretched.

Slowly my grandmother
picked up her basket
and cradled it into the house.

I asked trailing behind
Was it a baby grandma?
Was it really a baby?
She did not answer.
She did not close the door.
She held me and cried.

Holy Mess of a Girl

Oh, Dexter I'm such an unholy mess of a girl
—Katharine Hepburn in *Philadelphia Story*

Each night I take the poison, pinching off bits
of bitter memories. I'm testing to see if I am safe.
I dream of places like the oat field, the forest lane.
Wide open

able to see for miles where one lone oak tree,
a kind brother, stands in the middle of a field
where a farmer out of kindness kept it for shade
or some sort of mercy.

I could hide there. I live but carry death close. It's a
brittle seed, like Oleander or Hemlock tight in the pouch
of my mouth. It's like the bitter almond cyanide my German
ancestors hid in their pockets to escape their own horror.

I remember my mother's hands smelling
of Jergens lotion, cherries and almonds. I would lay
my head on her hands until the scent faded back
into sadness and tears.

Both of us broken by her father.

Out across the corn field a tumultuous fog is rolling in,
a tumor of a storm. Always convinced it could
come again for me like when he raped me.

I wonder if the wings I once grew would
again, lift me into a thousand clouds,
up in a flight past the crooked ceiling
tiles out beyond the dust, out the window.
Gone.

Long ago I was young and held my body
tight like a flint. I stopped scrubbing and
cleaning up after his sins. I became
a messy girl that no one wanted to touch.

I was a safe wilted rose, dirty, prickly
walking in the delicious freedom of rock,
dirt, deep in the field of my body.

Still at night when I enter the dark of sleep
I can no longer keep away winged terror.
It comes like those strange moths
I've heard of that come to sip tears, trying to
drink away the grief of my innocence lost.

The weak lines, of the projector are clicking clicking
each frame a screen on the back of my tired brain.
What he did, what she did, how they
looked away in Jesus' name.

The morning light comes with the weeping of doves.

Wash Away the Poet in Me

Wash my feet mother
off the juicy green
of mown grass
off the dusty lane
corn field dirt
off the silky sand.

Wash them, please,
back to innocence.

Time for clean stiff sheets
little girl long legs slide
in-between the cool cocoon.

Cry yourself to sleep mother
for the long drawn
out years of waiting
for your daughter to be
a cheerleader, homemaker,
innocent sister you tried to create.

Tell me, mother, were there years you
smiled?

Daughter of Enigma

I will pick & choose
my sorrows carefully
call down weather
wind or fog
dance on the mounds
of my dead & lost vices.

I am an unguarded
stepdaughter
falling from the grace
of a good life
tumbling off the hands
of the creator, a silent
Goddess of small truths
and I am falling
falling.
And I tell you
oh poor mother
oh poor father
oh poor poor
waiting family
there is no floor
no foundation
no end
for a poet.

Healer

I imagine myself back at the lake.
A tiny girl with fairy wings,
a chopped bowl haircut,
sprinkle of freckles,
sun dancing on my cheeks,
squinting at the lake's glint.

My job was to pull the hooks
out of the fish my
boy cousins caught
on bamboo
poles.

My medicinal aids,
gentle voice, seaweed
and water buckets to
heal the little yellow sunfish
with worried eyes and silky scales.

I'd take them aside to talk
about their journey
how tiny they were,
asking if things
were smoother down
in the warm murky waters
then where I stood.

Ten set free
two floated giving up
as they hit the water,
but not the yellow one.

I still can see her flash,
she who swallowed
the hook and lived.

The Understanding

When was it that
I became swallowed alive by poetry.

When did its deep gulp of
Wing scoop me up and

Carry me like a whistle
Through the trees.

A piece of loose paper spinning dancing.
I think it was that day, as a child,

I walked my mothers
Chihuahua.

He wanted to leap into the cool
Summer day.

To run run run
In circles breathing in

Panting out life.
I kept thinking about

The circle of life how everything
Made sense in that

Spinning truth.
The giant chestnut tree cradle over us.

The ancient air made of molecules.
Taking in a breath of Leonardo DaVinci

Tecumseh, Sylvia Plath, Madame Curie.
Eternal atoms, the death dust of ancient

Sisters and brothers. Later I would sit on
A slash of granite and find a perfectly

Carved prehistoric sword tip, the hand of
My ancestors reaching out of the soil
saying yes, yes.

When the Raven Came

The raven's wing was so close to my head
the swooshing split my being wide open.
Like an unexpected christening,
the gray air of angels.

Nothing has been the same since.

I am here now with air and earth
under a wing of gratitude
sitting in trees covered
with mossy fur watching.

My eyes transport my body
into all things
beginning and ending.
A full view of the world
birthing, the grave,
both an equal struggle.

The river, the dirty bank,
wild daisies.
The green things eaten.
The meat and the bone.

The shame that is required to kill to live.
Without this great misery we are lost.

There will not be bread upon
the water
nor a small
hand of a god, that dips into some
luminescent pool
to heal you.
Salvation is walking through it.

No matter how good, angry or pleasant
that relief is that you did not
have to suffer
like another.
The same waits for you
it comes to you as all

great sorrow
        loss
            terror comes
whether you feel it in your bones or flesh
or you watch it with your tired eyes.

It comes to pull you into the meat of life.
Place you slanted into the deep water.
Baptism and release.

See there out of the corner of your eye?
The small bird lights
on that branch.
It has known far more sorrow
than you and sings.

Stone

They are all innocent until proven guilty. But not me.
I am a liar until I am proven honest
                    —Louise O'Neill, *Asking for It*

As dangerous as a hand without a stone.
As dangerous as a stone without a hand.
Far heavier is a stone on the tongue of grief.

One is destruction
One is love
One is hunger.

One is my sister, your sister
One is my brother, your brother
One is my mouth trying to swallow.

As dangerous as a hand without a stone
As dangerous as a stone without a hand
Far heavier is a stone on the tongue of sorrow.

One is my sisters married to love.
One is me being raped my husband.
One is a heavy stone of truth

dropping from my mouth now that he's dead.

No one cares. Not family or children.

In the retched desert
on a quilt in the forest
in a house hidden on a hill

there is always this stone
on top of my body
where you left it

so, I'd forever be
mounted by fear and
your shame.

And now that you're dead
my sons hold the stone
carrying on the ancestral rage.

Too Many Angels

I want to watch the children as they run / Through the broken years /
I want this darkness gone . . . / . . . But there's no end in sight /
Only the dead of night / And too many angels . . .
—Jackson Browne

Inside me, there, in the corner are my little girls.
All these years they still wait for me to save them.

They're back in the 70s, in flower dresses,
tank tops, orange pedal pushers,

cherub lipped, popsicle-streaked arms, tricycle,
tiny bracelets and scraped knees.

They climb the swing set like a watch tower always
afraid grandfather will come with his hungry lap and fingers.

They wait on the hill of the field looking into the hope of the
summer sky where the starlings and crows' row row toward
heaven.

They play in the sandbox shoveling grained terror
into cracked pails, rusty pans preparing an inedible feast.

Sometimes I gather them in dreams trying to soothe them,
but a few slippery leap away using their tiny wing sprouts.

That one wants to jump off the bridge of my dreams.
Some are grown, silent. All of them a city built for survival.

Hands, an army of baby hands are so busy building a wall of stone
courage, a battlement from certain death.

Always the hope if it collapses someone
might say 'oh look she has been struck down,

let's pick her up' like in the movies where the ambulance comes,
and everyone cares. There what feels bad is bad.

There you can tell the truth. They want to know your truths,
because after all you're in a movie where everyone is seen
and heard.

At the end everyone discovers who the villain is and how he looks
like a good guy.

Weeks before he died at 86, he told me he was sorry for what he'd
done to me.

He said he could not stop, he saw me in the crib and loved me
too much.

Scherenschnitte

(Scissors cut)

My grandmother let me use
her scissor
when I was 8.

It was the sharp scissor.
She let me cut.
She knew I needed to cut.

I was the one no one
loved, except
she loved me.

My grandmother gave me the long
pointy scissors
and I cut out of one
white piece of paper

gnarled trees, vine,
grasses,
a sad deer, a bird flying
down to
the ground.

My grandmother gave me the scissor
so I could cut and cut and cut
so she could
praise me for cutting.

I knew she wanted
to show me there
would someday be a new life
away from my mother.

My grandmother gave me
the heaviest
scissor she had
the one that sat in
the wooden ducks head.
The one the grownups used.

The jabbing scissors.
My mother said it would poke out my eye.
The scissors few touched high
up on the refrigerator.

My grandmother handed me
a way out
to cut away the pain,
the nightmares.

When I was finished
she glued the lacy white
pieces on
thick red
construction paper
and called it beautiful,
extraordinary
and I knew
I someday could cut out
a life wild, free.

My Father Is the Moon Tonight

(For my father Jerry)

I can hear him say in my ear
put your coat on daughter or you'll get cold.

All night he shines
on me with a red planet proudly at his flank.

He is smiling serenely, finally steady.
He is not alone in the universe of the dead.

All night outside my window coyote's keen
a song of how he pulled himself up out of his old bones

and flew into the moon.

This night, with its icy wind
trees creaking voices in my ear, my father reaches

to hold me and each beam sliding shimmering is
his arms of light weaving through the black Locust trees.

When he decided he wanted to die he asked me
when I die will Jesus be there to greet me?

I told him he'd see his family, my mother would meet him,
but I knew it would be far greater than that.

I knew because he was a magical father
a child always of everything

he'd become light, stardust, moondust, bird wing,
a god to moths who fly up to him each night
finding their place called home

as I will someday be folded into that light too
in the arms of his light
past those dark locust trees to home.

Connected

In our effort to be so separate
in our effort to be the Hydrangea or orchid
not the Boxwood or plank
not the Sparrow rather a Flamingo

not the river
but the ocean

we trickle.

A fallen tree limb
raw joints ripped by a winter wind
stiff on the earth.

I did not see it suffer
I did not believe it was dying

because in Spring it sprouted.
Did it not know it was dead?

Thick twisted candy of a bud
uncurled into lush pink baby hands

reaching out
not following the bodies inclination to die
or maybe not having the understanding
of that letting go.

Just like my mother
for months she was dying in the late morning,
but would rise up fully each afternoon
because my father
begged her not to die.

Who begged this limb?
The brother grasses
saying see I am like you
I am still here after the harsh winter.

This tender innocence
of love and desire as one.

Of Mercy and Mercilessness

My palm grasps the smooth branch.
At dawn it was nibbled by a young deer
who has crossed the river looking for spring buds.

I am in the grasses, horsetail lace, tiny beaded
oat grass, two yellow puckered lipped
scotch broom watches me, and a strange large leaf maple
lays out its palms to me.

In the house a field away the news is on the TV
far off, yet always surrounding me.
This world churns up its old deceit into new colors.

Unharnessed mouths of hatred,
tongues of demons wagging fire,
all for them hungry to climb up onto a false throne,
but I am in the grasses with mosses,

rooted fists on rock and dirt with certainty.
I will hear the low thrush call, the certainty of spittle bugs
clump of foam with secret nymphs.

I am mud booted and ready, here not there
I am solid no dread. I have known the pain of loss
and survival in all its harshness that is gentler
then that of waring men.

As for nature the flowing seasons, it
has its own cruelty to bear.
I've seen it this Spring when the

tiny baby Merganser was swept down the river
from its mother off, away, alone
forever down down the churning
rocky river.

When Angels Sing

Did you know when angels sing
it's a foghorn
of a 1000 harmonies.
Close in your ear at night
so near you cannot move.

The tickling buzz is
authenticities stretch
deep inside.

If you rise you are
dizzy & captured
by an intention
to walk new pathways.

For days you'll long
to see a lone feather
floating
by your bed.
You will not it.

What I am telling you is
the ships at sea
are not closer to god
then we
each of us here
in this
fog sailing.

The Humming Light

It's cancer
you say

and I can hear a hum
in the background it's whispering
I'm dying.

That same damn
hum of hard truth just like
when we were kids.

How once in a moment
of true confession

I told you I was in love with a girl.
You told me you liked boys.
How alone we were then

in that backwoods world
where cheerleaders and jocks
were pregnant and married by 18.

In a world all about crops and cows
we were the unspoken shadows.

So many like us denied love
the old uncles and aunties alone.
The should and should nots of love,

because Jesus wouldn't like it.
Now again it's here
that same goddamn hum

uncontrollable,
ripping open the earth

under our feet into the unknown,
replete with sorrow
the worse sort of pain.

A rebellion now of our bodies
trying to deny again who we are.

Remember when we would

paint watercolors at my parents
house dreaming of being

famous, of being cool.
Escaping that shallow world
of basketball games

prom kings and queens.
One night I remember asking
you how to do shading in a painting.

You said look where the light falls
and since then, I have never stopped.

My dear brother, my soulmate friend
I cannot stop looking, I cannot
even comprehend

living life here
without you showing me when I fall
that I am light

without being in the wonder of your light.

Requiem

The last week in April you were
in the hospital room at the end of the hall.
One of the old rooms with chipped paint,
dirty scuffed floors. The place they
hide you when they can do no more.

I stood looking out the window
at the crashing waves of the lake.
The gritty glass and tiny flakes of snow.
My face like a moth in denial pounding
pounding to be set free from your dying.

When I touched your cold cheek,
kissed your open mouth
you whispered no more kisses
I don't want you to get this.
And a rawness rose up in my throat
an acid I knew I would
never be able to swallow down
with any sort of widow's grace.

I did not know how to do it
how to be the good wife with
my throat begging my tongue to speak.

My tongue rose up soft
like a deer asking can I drink from
this stream for you? Can I lay my palm
here on your head? Can I go in your place?

Instead, I asked if I could sing for you and
a lullaby like a silk ribbon rose up and

out of my throat into a longing
to sing you away from death.
You said no singing,
but that was all there was for me to do,
the damn song, the desire to sing
like some pied piper calling to your soul
stay, stay.

A Widow Waiting

I am the real thing.
That new neighbor who just became
a widow sobbing in her yard.

In the mornings I am
talking to my dead husband
telling him loudly I can't do this
I can't ride through this.

I am that woman all the town folks
talk about, we were that couple
that bought the house
on the corner.

Cars slow down
like our house
is a new circus come to town.
They all heard the story

how we came here so you could retire.
You were going to sail, I was going to write,
and how you died 3 weeks later.

In the morning I am a stiff salty
pillar standing by the lake
looking back at every moment.
Squinting, waiting for your boat,
certain this evening you will be standing

tall on the deck after a day of sailing,
how I will have my feet in the sand,
the wind playing with that summer dress.

At night I hear your voice calling me.
I jump up to help you and only find oxygen tanks.

I sob on the tile floor this place of dreams lost.
My tears like blood.

I want to fill this damn lake with tears,
I want to kill the fish and seaweed with my harsh red salt.
I can feel myself rolling off the end of the earth.

I am the woman who walks each day
to the veteran's memorial with our brown dog
talking to myself, praying and cursing wars,
begging the red path and stones with their
tiny name plaques Joseph, Allen, James,
to bring you back home.
I just want you home.
I repeat this mantra to the oaks.

I am the women in the store buying
one apple, one potato, looking like raggedy Anne
with all of my seams opened,
red yarn of my hair tumbling down.
All the dark inner stuffing falling out
of me and I don't care.

The elderly widow across the street
who lost her husband to the Korean war
stands at her door watching me
out in the harsh lake wind.

She watches me fall in my yard
to my knees.
She listens to my young widow sobs.
She wants to hold me, but turns away
knowing it must be this way.

Handless, alone in her kitchen, she pours tea.

The House That You Built for Me

Union is as if in a room there were two large windows
through which the light streamed in; it enters
in different places but it all becomes one.
                              —Saint Teresa of Avila

Each window in this house is
a window of forgiveness.

Each door a new hope or old security.

Hurry, come now
someone ask me how this is possible

after all, you are dead.

No one will understand my answer
that you are still here as you promised.

I am your formidable wife forever.

Not the kind of wife that lives
in a strange country of sparrow and hawks.

Nor the wife of a fisherman.

Nor the tired wife of a butcher man
cleaning up the strange curdling blood hourly.

Not the worn out by puns wife of a car salesman

or the suspicious wife of an artist
waiting for the model to leave.

I Am the wife of your death
the redemption, the falling into a journey
we all will take, but no one knows to where.

Each closet is wide open

with everything tumbling out
it's belly full of troubled thoughts open to all.

The yard a tangle of vines and leaves

worn old planks. Transgressions cast aside
the river is raging white and rampant.

The snow here is pure.

The rain cold deliciously slippery
each lick is the taste of sacred blood

the shiver, the rocks all tuned perfectly.

Millipedes, rolling bugs, worms
all another nature

all redeeming, grinding, working.

Each window in this house is
a window of forgiveness

I see through the glass clearly

not as they have said how it must be
for here there is no sin.

Lost at Sea

There must be something strangely sacred in salt.
It is in our tears and in the sea.

—Khalil Gibran

1

Always again the oceans next wave.
The sand, thinning beneath my feet.

I'm giving it my sadness
to carry away
sweeping out beyond the ships
into better storms.

I am trying with each step to
catch the bursts of foam
like its kiss can replace you.

I accept it's coming and going
it has its reasons,
you never really did.

Go slower I whisper
as it laps me
go
slower please . . .
don't forget me
when you rush out.

When you forgot me
I wanted to be swallowed
away slipping into a tide of indifference
longing for a fever that compelled me
to move forward
move forward.

2

I was born on the Great Lakes.
There is no salt or tide there.

The water often sits with a steady
stillness
at the shoreline
then gives a lazy roll

of meditation to rock and sand.

When winter comes it's a
burgeoning lover with
biting winds.
There is no more authentic love
as it breaks the body
as it tears boats apart.

It builds with its passion
icy sculptures over
lighthouses, against the shore.
Painting painting whatever is there
in a sweet rhythm of passion.
Tucking each object
into its arms of ice.

3

I was born in a shifty green hospital
smelling of my mother's ether.
The black and white habits
hanging over us as

I was pulled out with cold metal
clamps. Nuns washed me from
my mother's blood and caul.
It was the last time
I'd be so close to her or God.

4

I stand at this ocean and think of how
spring rains are melting the ice
far away
on the lake where I was born.

Its warm tongue tasting
the shore and piers
freeing them up to live again.

I came to the Pacific later in my life
as if it was my mother
it terrified me and I loved it
for that terror.

The water, a salty brew,
I drink from its womb
always trying to enter deeper and deeper
curled into its enraptured arms.

Siren Song (After Your Death)

When you go to bed, don't leave bread or milk
on the table: it attracts the dead
—Rainer Maria Rilke, *Sonnet 6, From Sonnets to Orpheus*

Most days I search for your eyes
like I lost my glasses. I search faces
in the crowd like I am a child who's lost
their parent in the grocery store.
I am a lost dog on the highway checking
each car as it speeds by searching
for my home.

At night, the shuffle of wind, storms tossing,
there is no unearthing of you.
Even in my deepest slumber I wake
my arms stretched out across your pillow,
my hand clutching it like I used to clutch
your tee-shirt when we would sleep.

You call my name at night out of a deep sleep.
Calling me to the lake shore where the sails
of our dreams float.
I watch them white, billowing, moving
away from the shore, from me.

The black swans following, circling
carrying them out across the endless sea.
I cry into silence, into emptiness.

What can I do to lure you back?
The simple candle burning each
night by the window.
A door left open, often slammed
closed by a wind of sorrow.

A small white saucer of milky words.
The milk and bread of a failing, a bitter
brave letting go.
I ask only one thing, how does
one call back the pieces,
those parts of me, that traveled
with you into your deep winter?

Your Steady Partner

I rub my hands down your thighs
and breathe in your sweet mystery
claiming this moment as mine.
Climbing it wildly like a vine into your heat.

I take from you like no other
this I know and Jesus could not
taste nor your plain simple lover
the dark tangy music that's on my tongue.

Oh yes, she cooks dinner, her apron tight
and tidy, hair up in a bow. The essence
of cotton candy and play dough
Oh, she was an easy one for your mold.

You and I our desires keep good company
each detail we pamper and seduce
small phantoms that we must
love as our bodies love.

On the radar in the pulsing air
she is the tiny black spot that says
home and going back you will plan
time to sail away from her again.

I am that foreign place, that strange laughter
in the other room. The tiny mumbling voice you swear
you can hear talking far off in the night
when you try to sleep, but ache for clear words.

I do not wear a watch and that was true for you once.
I read dictionaries and thrill to the thesaurus.
We have familiar things Vivaldi, Bartlett's quotations
and all other simple elements of disorder.

She tucks you in, baths each dish
like a soiled child, Facebook posts
about baking bread, drinking wine.
She opens her plump thighs
warm and milky to you
when you have that sharp
need to bed me.

And I am, my darling,
oh, so far away
from where you are.
So far and wide open and clever,
oh, so clever to be a
deliciously faint indiscretion, so free.

Moonlight

(To Stephen flying in Prudhoe Bay)

I am thinking in the dark morning about
the moon we knew in Alaska or moons
everywhere, every place.

Like the moonlight racing through
the woods last night. Slanted tail of silken
light dodging in and out between
the legs of crystal trees. Bright beams
jogging off blue snows quiet rest.

Then there is a monster of an orange
crumbly moon the tip of its belly
slowly sinking behind red castles of rock
and spirit in Sedona.

Or the moon you see on clefted Arctic Sea
ice that trails a million miles infinity round.
The place that never settles your heart
only moments on the journey are home.

Alone I stood at the window last night in
the light of a whole full moon, ripe and ready.
I wanted to be whole, round lusty here,
naked to black skies everywhere, everyplace.

The Thistle Flower

I want to grow artichokes for you.
Bristly and heavy headed with their
purple tongues flicking the air.

I want to be the scent of butterflies
like we smelled on the mountain
as we climbed into Spring.

I want to pull off the Ponderosa
pine bark pieces sliding each puzzle
piece into the other to build a path
for you to climb back to me.

The river is rolling slowly.
Perfect its steady quiver
at the lip of the bank.

The pairing faultless, tight up against
the edge turning it greener greener,
pressing grasses into a sway.

I'm a red poppy in my last summer breeze
waiting for you to collect me
to shimmer my yellow desire.
Your touch the dilation to my furled petals.

If you asked me, I'd be your whore, your saint,
your prophetess. I'd sing hymns, honky-tonk
tunes, or songs about mountains climbed,
prairies crossed and sacred rivers tumult.

All this I'd do to flip you
over onto your feet out of the shell

of shame and back into the lubricious
greed we once had for each other's
bodies and minds with its rising,
falling and wet exchange.

I want to grow artichokes for you.
Heavy headed and swollen,
their taste sweet, bitter and
the memory of the swell of you as they globe.

The Label

You were surprised that I saw
the small morsels you were leaving
along the way. A trail of regret
wrapped up to look like romance.

The perfume you gave me
the black bottle cool, metallic,
clicking "release me" against
my rings when
I opened it.

The scent
crumbs of black velvet,
tired rose petals,
holy church incense,
cedars powdered resins,

stiff lilies of a funeral home.

The label read
Mourning.

Impossible Love

Under the Night sky
A tiny
Orchid among
Moss and stones
—Robert Carpenter

When you saw me with the ravens,
heard me speak with them
in a forest far from home

their answers opened you wide,
swam through your body.
I saw the wave of it
how you tasted
your body becoming
more a part of you
and then the closing down again.

Out into the speckled light
first stream
leaves floating into their letting go.
We with a ripe harvest stirring
in silence between us.

Like the time the dead spoke
through me to you
even though death for you was
the greatest horror,

you listened.

How am I to forget
the power of that love.
You swallowed the world
of my mystery
drinking it through you.

Then your silence
the rush to frost,
to an early winter.

There, the impossible
is comfortable, no trying,
no explanation, no fear that
it will collapse you down into
the old terror and need
to run   to run   from loving.

Even now after so long
you stay
like your heart is a ghost
unable to leave me.

A Thousand Pieces of My Heart

One morning, I found two
Varied Thrush dead, laying side by side
outside the greenhouse.

It was as if they dived into love, and it killed them.
That glass house, was the only place that
felt like home to you.

I'd watch you through the window tenderly
bed broken leaves of succulents into pots
the size of your thumbs.

I believed in signs, warnings of things to come.
At its door overnight sprouted
translucent Indian Pipes.

They rose out of the crumbly soil
like alien question marks or ruffled
ended shepherds' staffs.

It was as if they asked, do you know who I am,
will you love me like you loved the rose or lily,
will you pick me, vase me,

or will you discard me wary that
I may poison you
with my strange ways.

One night you came through the door
with a waltz playing on your phone.
You placed it on the coffee table,

taking me up into your arms,
dancing me around the living room
and time felt infinite, this yes, this.

Later you stood at the foot of the bed
and announced like a schoolboy
that you wanted to sing a song for me.

When you did, a thousand pieces of my heart
gathered together for the first time in my life,
stirring you into my forever.

Sometimes at night, I still want your back
your hip, freckled shoulders, sandy colored skin,
the way you'd say 'tuck in tight'

and I'd place my face into the warmth
between your shoulder blades wondering
if you were starting to turn

away, if you had met her, someone better,
if you were dreaming of her younger landscape
not the old desert of me.

I believed if you left me for another, left then came
back to me, left then came back to me, you'd realize
I was the best and that you were for me and I for you.

You told me the first time you saw
my photo you fell in love
with my sadness.

When you loved me all my sadness disappeared.
When you would leave me, it returned.
How many times did you create my sadness

to love me again? I did not count.
I only know you finally found someone else
whose sadness was more beautiful than mine.

Fairy Tales Simply Put

As you get older you realize
there are things that really do happen
like maybe Red Riding Hood did spend
sometime near the belly of a wolf.

She was young, naïve, but felt safe pinned
to the inside of the intestine, near the kidney.
at first it had to hurt the biting,
chewing, the gulp of a swallow,
but then the respite from responsibility
had to be nice.

I was captured once by a man
whose balls moved like an animal
in their hairy pouch all night long.
I know this because he pinned me
to his pelvis, there I stayed unable to
look up into his yellow eyes.

I was a Rapunzel looking down
at her freedom
with hapless sorrowful eyes
with so little to drop for redemption.
At night the old dwarf of my crackled anger,
my fever and prayers
spun kind words out of my tears
which each morning

I offered to the wolf
as penance for still being so alive.

White Swans

. . . I saw twelve angels wheeling in the sun, rays
of white wings and gold light . . . Swans!
—Maxine Hong Kingston

Pull me into the white swans
streaming
grace, grace and grace.

Let me be simply
a poet watching
from the shore
a wedge of white swans
floating
on slate
November water.

Let this be

a release of longing.

I fall into nothing
just this
the perfect swans.

Pull me into the gray
where everything
is waiting for me
the stillness,
running light tracing a shoreline.

My longing is without a wish,

it's a plastic bag tangled
on a branch blowing
in the wind never sturdy

with the
trembling
bones of pleasure.

Let me lay

in the reeds
and grasses
arms of soft mercies
their hollow
whistle of blessings.

Here on solid land
I try my best to be free
from closed
tumbling in my
steel basket of belief.

This morning
I look out to the waters
hungry,
longing, hoping,
the white swans will
unfold
themselves and

scoop me

up

into a flight of surrender
into the icy air

away

from the storm
of your
death.

Untangled

All of our stuff
was tangled together

like our eyes when we met
legs, arms each finger lonely

and loosened. All our paintings,
books, kitchen herbs, photos

and words that can't be undone
stuck in the lubricious agony of love.

There will never be an undoing
of this in me.

There will never be an
easiness with this.

There will never be a door or window
cracked open in me again.

The feather you found,
the leaf I caught in the morning light.

Words and words and midnight whispers.
Early Sunday morning gamble of confessions.

Trying to be me was too hard to take on.
I cannot bear myself day after day.

You cannot bear my excavating you.
I prefer voices, you, silence.

You once said you needed
to flow with the river.

I told you I needed to stand firm
in the current. Too often I let

myself be taken by anothers river
where love has journeyed

down from me, away
into tangled uncertainty

The weeds, rocks of you are loosened
flowing with your new love
down her river.

Full Whole Moon

Last night I woke in slow
milky moonlight, head to toe
it was making love to me.

I became effervescent glowing
with its soft blanket hands.
They settled here
and there in the room of my life.

All night it stroked my body while I slept
from window-to-window satiating
its ceaseless hunger.

I want to tell you this because,
you have left me. I want you
to feel it with me
so you understand
how it is to persist in loves light.

How it came to me fully, no judgments,
wanting only me and entered me
undiluted no shame or fear.

How it laid next to me naked, stirring
its breath like the owls call
swooping
without hesitation, without a sound.

Last night you slept with her
in your shallow dark bed
having forsaken our love.

But the moon has enraptured me
full and bright in its passion.
It never wavered once in its embrace.

All night long the full whole moon
greater more immense without a body
its light made love to me

and I am changed.

The Waves of the Bay

(Homer, Alaska)

1

Seagulls are bright sparks of white
flickering through the spraying rich dark sky
rising up out of the deep blue of Katchemak Bay.

Now shifting, bobbing on the water
stiff little puppets watching, waiting for the suns
thick descent into the closing mouth of the day.

At night they are little bits of stars
bobbing on the belly of the water, plunging their heads
between the peaceful thighs of the waves.

2

Tonight, out on this balcony I suffer the pulse of you
washing in and out and thru me
there is only this and that moment.

Remembering how once I laid my head on your thigh
crying down the length of it because I knew
we would never have such hunger again.

3

Leaving you there was a soft madness that pushed
its stake down my tired spine.
I had forgotten the mornings passing

the sunny flowers on a white crisp tablecloth
and overhead the damn sound of the seagulls
crying for me because I have no more tears for this.

Tonight, I can only blink at a small distant light across this bay,
which you have never known, and off in the distance
there is a sort of luminous transparency rolling gently this way.

Do You Know How Dangerous It Is

to think about someone's hands?
It takes you into the secret places where they live.

Hands slicing, stroking, sorting, pointing
instantly you are clenched in their sweaty fists.

Once I cradled and kissed the palm of a hand that had
just touched the hard nipple of my breast.

The same day I shook the smooth limp
hand of a pastor after Easter service.

My father had the hard tired hands of a truck driver.
My mother the silky weak hands of a madwoman.

One time I held the tear scented hand of a whore.
Her bright purple stars painted on each nail tip cried redemption.

I have wiped tenderly clean the tiny starfish
hand of an infant reaching up and out
to an unknown world.

But your hands your hands travel.
Each a strong engine pulling, rope pulling
sailing, traveler out into this world.

Strong and brave they are dumb to disparaging events.
They are active with passion. A saxophone, a guitar,
a piano, a sailboat, a helicopter and a strange woman's silky flesh.

Your hands travel as hands do and so follows the heart.

Finding My Way Home

I miss the thicket
the wicker of those baskets
made of willow.
The tiny birds
in the brush
darting.
I cannot find
a place where I am not
restless.

The only home
I had was
when I was understood
by you.

So I look in the back yard
of each person I meet.
Wanting the light to be
stretched out long,
the snow to fall for hours,
the sound of cars passing
on a faraway road,
the dawn to call us out
to explore gritty truck stops
and coffee simmered all night,
and the porch light
that still hopes
you find your
way home.

When the World Stops for Wonder

It's Spring and there's a little girl walking with
her grandfather and a Bassett hound in the early morning light.

She is talking nonstop about each of the wonders she
is seeing on this ordinary day. Grass, pebble, stone.

It is like that for old souls when they return to earth again
into a new time and new place.

It is worth death to come back to the fresh
face of the world.

She's squatting to watch the dog sniff the grass and hydrant
watching his wrinkled face and laughing.

All the while her grandfather is in a sleepy daze
stumbling ahead with the leash in his hands.

She is in a wonder picking at the tree and seeing
the tiny ants on a flower.

She is delight, everything delight,
I transform into delight simply watching her.

Today on this old street in a shabby neighborhood
on a cool early Sunday suddenly, the world opens to me

with cherry blossom petals
apple blossom petals their flight my baptism.

As she follows her grandfather back into the house
she squats to look at the mosaic of stones in the driveway

picking two to put in her pocket
to carry her wonder along with her all day.

This gift of fresh sight she has given to me
the memory of her now two glorious stones in my pocket.

The Harvest

What's in the length of this poem?
How far in will the roots reach?
How far up will the stalks grow?
Or will it die
as I have allowed
so many things I love
to die before.

It is a seed to me
a tiny oily pod
filled with the rich
head of harvest dreams.

It carries me, this poem,
to the stories of my ancestors
that I have wrapped my
feet in so I could
dance the dance of my people
so that I could breathe and
follow a good solid road
to home.

The Light of Home at the End
of the Gravel Road

Down the gravel road to the waxy yellow
light into the barn, into the milkhouse.
Pitchfork, shovel, an eager empty pail.

Lines of cows are walking in from the pasture
seeking the barns light. Necklace of white faces,
soft faces moving toward it and the sweet hay.

What is it in our animal bodies that calls generations
home at dusk? The hunger for that yellow smudge of light.
The silent dusk welcomes you into the arms of home.

Something in our core wants that glow,
the windows watching us come and go, the eyes of place.
The worn kitchen table, the bowl, the spoon, the fire.

The dog greeting you as if there was nothing greater
in his day than you coming home.
And now you can let fall away and away
the heaviness of the world.

The bed the sheets white as a new day.
Listening to the wind as the snow tumbles
creating deep waves into the fields.

Dreaming of far-off places and a good solid loneliness
that wraps you in your small room, the cradling
of the simple family, the sequestering of blizzard
as it natters, rushes, covers.

And no matter where you are deep down in city lights
or flying to some foreign place
just the thought of being home on the farm

you become a child again. The one who lives
in the stone house, the silent light,
with the happy dog, pleasant cows, the rolling hills,
the one at the end
of the gravel road.

About the Author

J.V. Foerster was born in Port Washington, Wisconsin. She is published internationally appearing in many literary magazines including *Cirque, Eclectica, Burningword Literary Journal, Amethyst Review, Quartet, The Field Guide Magazine, The Bluebird Word, The Fiery Scribe, Green Ink Press, Loch Raven Review, Agnieszka's Dowry,* and *Horsethiefs Journal,* to name a few. She has work in multiple anthologies and was a finalist in the Oprelle Poetry contest. She has also won three honorable mentions from the Oregon State Poetry Association. J.V. is a three-time Pushcart nominated poet. She was a cocreator of the play *Between Night Dreams and My Life.*

J.V. is also a published painter and photographer. She worked using poetry therapy and art therapy in a healthcare setting. She also worked with abused children and their parents in a Childrens Advocacy Center in Alaska.

She lives in Ashland, Oregon.

Made in the USA
Monee, IL
02 September 2023

42024006R00049